LABELS AND TAGS

ROCKPORT
PUBLISHERS

Rockport Publishers, Inc.
Gloucester, Massachusetts

£14.99

First published in the United States of America by:
Rockport Publishers, Inc.
33 Commercial Street
Gloucester, Massachusetts 01930-5089
Telephone: (978) 282-9590
Facsimile: (978) 283-2742

Distributed to the book trade and art trade in the United States by:
North Light Books, an imprint of
F & W Publications
1507 Dana Avenue
Cincinnati, Ohio 45207
Telephone: (800) 289-0963

Other Distribution by:
Rockport Publishers, Inc.
Gloucester, Massachusetts 01930-5089

ISBN 1-56496-508-2

10 9 8 7 6 5 4 3 2 1

Designer: SYP Design & Production
Cover crredits (clockwise from top left)
pages: 50, 46, 48, 72, 45, 52

Manufactured in Hong Kong.

INTRODUCTION

Steiff Teddy Bears, Levi's, Nike. . . . These universally recognized products and labels are a designer's dream—logos that caught on and passed the test of time. It is the products themselves that sell, but it's the logo that sustains the sales. In a department store, on a grocery shelf, or on a billboard, the logo is what makes the consumer get that "oh, there it is" look that makes all designers proud.

With only one or two sides to a label or tag, the challenge for the designer is optimizing the use of such limited space. Not only are labels and tags hindered by size, but their designs are only two-dimensional. Developing a logo that can be placed on a card or sewn onto an article of clothing needs to be small enough to fit, but head-turning to the consumer. The designers featured in this latest volume of the Design Library series, *Labels and Tags*, were able to succeed at this tricky task. Page through this rich visual resource and see for yourself how these catchy designs attract your eye.

DESIGN FIRM Love Packaging Group
ALL DESIGN Tracy Holdeman
CLIENT The Hayes Company
PRODUCT Amaryllis & Paperwhite Bulb Gardens
TECHNIQUE Offset

A folding carton stock "wrap" is used instead of a box, allowing the product's charm to show through. Illustrations were done with markers and colored pencils on plain copier paper. Old-fashioned illustrated stickers were added to the end panels and a raffia-ribbon accent and complimentary gardener's journal complete the package.

DESIGN FIRM Love Packaging Group
ALL DESIGN Tracy Holdeman
CLIENT The Hayes Company
PRODUCT Squirrel feeder
TECHNIQUE Flexography (two colors)

The client wanted a package that was unique, "down-home," and that clearly explained the product. Pencil sketches were enlarged, then scanned and placed in a layout in Macromedia FreeHand. The design required no trapping, only overprinting. The "corrugated corn" is produced in the "scrap" area of the cutting die, so the whole package can be produced in one pass in the manufacturing/printing process.

(opposite page)

PRODUCT Vinegar & Chutney
CLIENT Vaughn Weeden Creative Inc.
DESIGN FIRM Vaughn Weeden Creative Inc.
ART DIRECTOR Dan Flynn, Steve Weeden & Rick Vaughn
DESIGNER Dan Flynn
ILLUSTRATOR Bill Gethold

DESIGN FIRM DIL Consultants in Design
ALL DESIGN DIL Staff
CLIENT Cia. Cerveharia Brahma
PRODUCT Brahma soft drinks
TECHNIQUE Dry-offset printing

Aiming to promote its line of soft drinks during the months before the Olympic Games, Brahma solicited the designers to develop promotional cans. Each brand (Gurana, Sukita, and Limao) received a different design of an Olympic sport, especially the ones which had best chances of winning a medal for Brazil.

DESIGN FIRM Clark Design
ART DIRECTOR Annemarie Clark
DESIGNER/ILLUSTRATOR Thurlow Washam
CLIENT North Coast Coffee
PRODUCT Coffee
TECHNIQUE Offset

The client requested an upscale look with more sophistication than a coffee boutique, so Clark Design used metallic silver to add elegance and to match the silver bags that had to be used in packaging. It was created in QuarkXPress and Adobe Illustrator.

St. Honoré Moon Cake

DESIGN FIRM Alan Chan Design Company, Wanchai,
 Hong Kong

CREATIVE DIRECTOR Alan Chan

DESIGNERS Alan Chan and Phillip Leung

PHOTOGRAPHER Sandy Lee

DESIGN FIRM Wickens Tutt Southgate, London, England
ART DIRECTOR Mark Wickens
DESIGNER Simon Coker

Morgan's Spiced Rum label is screened directly onto
the glass

DESIGN FIRM Mires Design

ART DIRECTOR José A. Serrano

DESIGNER José A. Serrano, Miguel Perez

ILLUSTRATOR Tracy Sabin

CLIENT Found Stuff Paper Works

PRODUCT Stationery

The idea behind this project was to develop packaging that accomplished two purposes: (1) to convey the message that the product was made of 100 percent recycled materials, and (2) to create a sense of value for a product that was made of recycled products.

DESIGN FIRM Heather Sumners
ALL DESIGN Heather Sumners
CLIENT Bender's Beverage Co.
PRODUCT Non-alcoholic grape juice
TECHNIQUE Color pencil, typesetting

This label design for Bender's non-alcoholic grape juice was produced and created in QuarkXPress. The client wanted a clean, simple, classic design that would be timeless. The use of muted classic colors helped achieve that effect.

DESIGN FIRM JCHO
ALL DESIGN Juan Carlos, Hernández Ortega
CLIENT Mezcal JCHO
PRODUCT Mezcal
TECHNIQUE Paper, ink, rope, bottle

The designers glued rope around a bottle with a cork. They designed the label, cut it out, and glued it to the bottle, then designed a logo for the cork.

PRODUCT Eruc Boxes and Package Design
DESIGN FIRM Margo Chase Design
ART DIRECTOR-DESIGNER Margo Chase
CLIENT Ecru

(opposite page)
PRODUCT Packaging Design for Mandarin
  Oriental, The Flower Shop
CLIENT Mandarin Oriental, The Flower Shop
DESIGN FIRM Alan Chan Design Company
ART DIRECTOR Alan Chan
DESIGNER Alan Chan/Tsoi Chen Shun
ILLUSTRATOR Alan Cracknel

DESIGN FIRM Hornall Anderson Design Works
ART DIRECTOR Jack Anderson
DESIGNERS Jack Anderson, David Bates, Mike Courtney
CLIENT K2 Corp
PRODUCT K2 Goggle Packaging

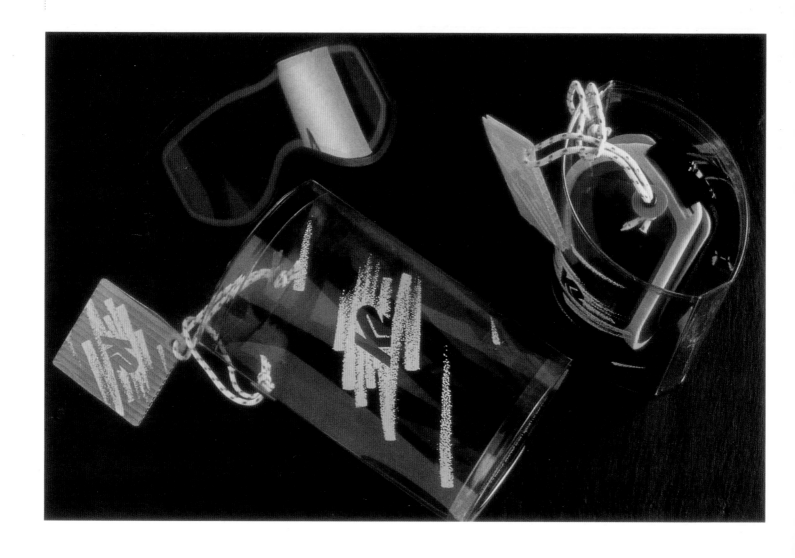

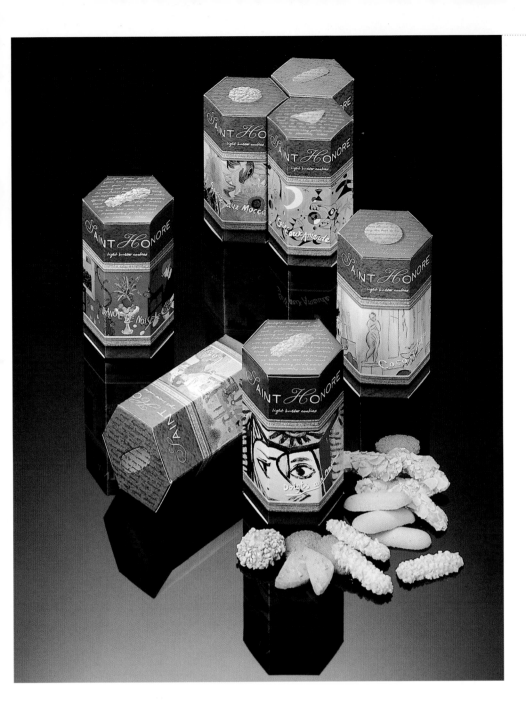

DESIGN FIRM Alan Chan Design Company
ART DIRECTOR Alan Chan
DESIGNER Alan Chan & Tsoi Chen Shun
PHOTOGRAPHER Sandy Lee
CLIENT St. Honore Cake Shop Ltd.
PRODUCT Packaging Design for St. Honore Cookies

DESIGN FIRM Alan Chan Design Company
ART DIRECTOR Alan Chan
DESIGNER Alan Chan, Phillip Leung, Peter Lo
CLIENT Asean Cuisine Ltd.
PRODUCT Packing Design for Mythical China & Family Kitchen

(opposite page)
DESIGN FIRM Newell and Sorrell, Ltd., London
CREATIVE DIRECTOR John Sorrell
DESIGNER Domenic Lippa

Packaging design for the Hot Bagel Company, London

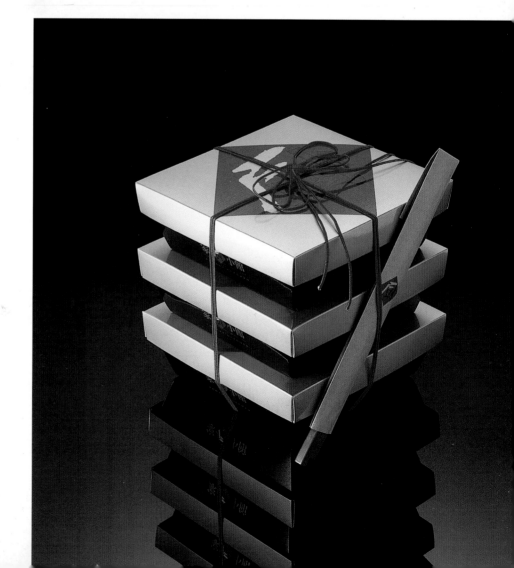

(opposite page)

DESIGN FIRM Olson Johnson Design Co.
ART DIRECTOR Haley Johnson
DESIGNER Haley Johnson
ILLUSTRATOR Haley Johnson
CLIENT Palais D'amour
PRODUCT Palais D'amour Honeymoon Sweet

DESIGN FIRM Mittleman/Robinson, Inc.
ART DIRECTOR Pam Robinson
CLIENT Kraft/General Foods
PRODUCT General Foods International Coffee
Annual Collectible Tins Series

DESIGN FIRM CMA
ART DIRECTOR Bob Milz
DESIGNER Leon Alvarado, Trish Hill
ILLUSTRATOR Jeff Sanson
CLIENT BRIK Toy Co.
PRODUCT Rods&Pods
TECHNIQUE Airbrush illustration, offset

Rods&Pods is a new product engineered to fit with and connect to all the other leading building block systems. The cylindrical cardboard tube packages show a construction built with the contents of that size package, and additional illustrations around the tube emphasize the compatibility of this toy.

DESIGN FIRM Rickabaugh Graphics
ALL DESIGN Eric Rickabaugh
CLIENT Nationwide Insurance Company
PRODUCT Insurance software
TECHNIQUE Offset

Life Manager software is used by Nationwide Insurance agents to create insurance projections for clients. Because it helps agents "juggle" client facts and figures, Rickabaugh Graphics created the juggler image and applied it to labels, manuals, packaging, and announcements.

DESIGN FIRM Curtis Design

ART DIRECTOR David Curtis

DESIGNER/ILLUSTRATOR Chris Benitez

CLIENT Nibbler Farms

PRODUCT Fresh cut produce

Turn-of-the-century style crate art is updated to give the packaging relevance in today's fresh cut produce category.

DESIGN FIRM

Del Rio Diseño

ART DIRECTOR/DESIGNER

Del Rio Diseño team

CLIENT

Carozzi

PRODUCT

San Remo pastas

TECHNIQUE

Rotogravure

This line has been redesigned to make the brand remind the consumer of Italy and its tradition in pastas. Strong diagonals and the colors of the Italian flag were used in the design to distinguish it from the competition.

DESIGN FIRM Pedersen Gesk
ART DIRECTOR Mitch Lindgren
DESIGNER Kris Morgan, Thom Middlebrook
CLIENT Arctco Industries
PRODUCT Arctic Cat

The brand mark created clearly captures the essence
of the brand and the attitude of the target
consumer. The black package demonstrates the
premium, high-tech quality of the products.

DESIGN FIRM Mires Design
ART DIRECTOR José A. Serrano
DESIGNER José A. Serrano, Miguel Perez
PHOTOGRAPHER Carl Vanderschuit
CLIENT Voit Sports
PRODUCT Basketball

Voit Sports was introducing a brand-new line of ball
with a unique grip. Mires Design selected a bold,
highly visible, and somewhat playful looking font. It
then manipulated the original font to emphasize the
energy of a three-dimensional sphere-shaped
product.

20

DESIGN FIRM Angelo Sganzerla

ART DIRECTOR/DESIGNER Angelo Sganzerla

ILLUSTRATOR Roberto Weikmann

CLIENT Stainer

PRODUCT Pralines, meringues, nougats

The illustrations for this children's package line are collages showing fantasy patterns or scenes evocative of Mexico, the land of cocoa's origin. The rear illustration shows the product, which is always cocoa-based.

DESIGN FIRM Angelo Sganzerla

ART DIRECTOR/DESIGNER Angelo Sganzerla

ILLUSTRATOR Alfonso Goi

CLIENT Stainer

PRODUCT Praline chocolates

A line of praline chocolates made with natural ingredients, such as orchard fruits and herbs, are illustrated with watercolors.

DESIGN FIRM Alan Chan Design Co.
ART DIRECTOR Alan Chan
DESIGNERS Alan Chan, Phillip Leung
ILLUSTRATOR Gary Cheung
CLIENT Hong Kong Seibu Enterprise Co. Ltd.
PROJECT HK Seibu Christmas Shopping Bag

DESIGN FIRM Lambert Design
ART DIRECTOR Christie Lambert
DESIGNER/ILLUSTRATOR Joy Cathey Price
CLIENT Duo Delights
PRODUCT Reindeer Feed (candy)
TECHNIQUE Offset

Reindeer Feed is white chocolate and nuts and is marketed during the holidays in catalogs and specialty stores. The concept was to make a hang tag that resembles a deer crossing warning sign, but with a red-nosed reindeer. All the art was created in Adobe Illustrator.

DESIGN FIRM Lippa Pearce Design Limited,
Twickenham, United Kingdom
DESIGNER Harry Pearce
PRODUCT Boots Repel Plus insect repellent

PRODUCT Boots Wart Remover, manufactured in
the United Kingdom
DESIGN FIRM Lippa Pearce Design Limited,
Twickenham, United Kingdom
DESIGNERS Harry Pearce and Domenic Lippa

DESIGN FIRM Tieken Design and Creative Services

ART DIRECTOR Fred E. Tieken

DESIGNER Fred E. Tieken, Rik Boberg

CLIENT Black Mountain Brewing Company

PRODUCT Juanderful Weizen beer

TECHNIQUE Offset

Because wheat beer was originally brewed by monks, the client wanted to convey an old-world, somewhat monastic message through the graphics. The woodcut-style illustrations of shocks of wheat and barrel add to the "made-by-hand" appeal. The lettering and graphics were created in Adobe Illustrator and imported into Adobe Photoshop and manipulated.

DESIGN FIRM Carter Wong and Partners Ltd.

ART DIRECTOR Philip Carter

DESIGNER Philip Carter, Teri Howes

CLIENT AC Water Canada Inc.

PRODUCT Crystal Canadian

TECHNIQUE Four-color process, lithography

The Maple Leaf was used to convey the Canadian origins with the expressed permission of the Canadian government. The simplicity of the color-coded label design illustrates the crisp, pure qualities of the water. Silver edging enhances the premium nature of the product. The label was created in Adobe Illustrator.

DESIGN FIRM Tieken Design and Creative Services

ART DIRECTOR Fred E. Tieken

DESIGNER Rik Boberg, Fred E. Tieken

CLIENT Black Mountain Brewing Company

PRODUCT Chili Light Beer

TECHNIQUE Label–offset, six-pack carrier–flexography

The client wanted to convey the same vibrant and colorful Southwestern image of its orginal product, so the designers used clouds and floating chilies to convey the "lightness" of this new product. The lettering and graphics were created in Adobe Illustrator and then merged with a CD-ROM photo image of clouds in Adobe Photoshop.

DESIGN FIRM Tharp Did It

ART DIRECTOR Rick Tharp, David Hansmith

DESIGNER/ILLUSTRATOR Rick Tharp

CLIENT Mount Konocti Winery

PRODUCT Mount Konocti Pear Brandy

TECHNIQUE Letterpress

The artwork for this label was handmade, as is the brandy. The label was letterpressed in four colors and applied by hand.

DESIGN FIRM Trickett & Webb

DESIGNERS Brian Webb, Lynn Trickett, Ian Cockburn

ILLUSTRATOR Trickett & Webb

CLIENT Anthony Green Pet Products

DESIGN FIRM Kollberg-Johnson Assoc.

ART DIRECTOR-DESIGNER Penny Johnson

CLIENT Ralston Purina

PRODUCT Whisker Lickins Cat Treats

DESIGN FIRM Murrie, White, Drummond, Lienhart

ART DIRECTOR-DESIGNER Jayce Dougall Schmidt

CLIENT Harper Leather Goods MFG Co.

PRODUCT Basted Dog Treats

PROJECT Series of tins for Alan Chan Creations Ltd.

DESIGN FIRM Alan Chan Design Company, Wanchai, Hong Kong

CREATIVE DIRECTOR Alan Chan

DESIGNERS Alan Chan, Alvin Chan and Phillip Leung

DESIGN FIRM CMA

ART DIRECTOR Bob Milz

DESIGNER Dave Campbell, Bob Milz

ILLUSTRATOR Bob Milz, Dave Campbell, Trish Hill

CLIENT Uncle Ben's Rice

PRODUCT Uncle Ben's Beans & Rice line

TECHNIQUE Macromedia FreeHand

For a new line of regional specialty beans and rice dishes, Uncle Ben's asked CMA to combine its corporate orange box look with a decorative illustrative element to romanticize the regional differences among the various beans and rice combinations.

DESIGN FIRM The Hive Design Studio

DESIGNER Laurie Okamura, Amy Bednarek

CLIENT K.J.B. Foods

PRODUCT Old Wharf Fish House brand specialty foods

TECHNIQUE Flexography

The "Old World Fishing Harbor" look in a "fishing crate" package was created by using Adobe Illustrator with a rubber stamped look. Burnt paper was scanned to create the old paper look on the labels.

DESIGN FIRM
FLB Design Ltd.
ART DIRECTOR
Colin Mechan
DESIGNER
Susan Fosbery
ILLUSTRATOR
Ian Mudie
CLIENT
Kraft Jacobs Suchard
PRODUCT
Maxwell House Instant Coffee Powder
TECHNIQUE
Lithography

An initial black-and-white illustration was produced to emulate the background swirl effect—this was then scanned into a Scitex system and manipulated to work around the type. A full-color illustration of the coffee beans was created to enhance the taste cues. Full digital artwork was produced using Adobe Illustrator. FLB then project managed the origination stage, which included production of films and wet proofs.

DESIGN FIRM
Westpoint Stevens Inc. design group
ART DIRECTOR
Gail Rigelhaupt
DESIGNER
Risa Brand
CLIENT
Westpoint Stevens Inc.
PRODUCT
Tea
TECHNIQUE
Offset

The labels of this promotional gift were developed using patterns from four of the company's major bedding collections. Each tea was chosen to relate to the concept of the collection (i.e., English Breakfast for a collection adapting a William Morris print, Chamomile, a calming tea, for the "weekend," and so on).

DESIGN FIRM Graif Design
ALL DESIGN Matt Graif
CLIENT Graif Design
PRODUCT Portfolio
TECHNIQUE Embossing, offset, color laser output

Looking for a unique way of presenting Graif Design's logos and illustrations, the designer discovered these plain looking cans and brought them to life with embossing and printing. They cost about $5 a piece to produce plus time to assemble.

DESIGN FIRM Graif Design
ALL DESIGN Matt Graif
CLIENT Graif Design
PRODUCT Beer
TECHNIQUE Embossing on silver metallic paper

The designer makes his own beer, so he created this package to showcase his package design ability. The entire piece was created in Adobe Illustrator. Labels are hand die-cut and applied. They cost $8 each to produce plus time to assemble.

DESIGN FIRM Alan Chan Design Design Co.
DESIGNERS Alan Chan, Alvin Chan
CLIENT Heichinrou Restaurant

DESIGN FIRM Alan Chan Design Co.
ART DIRECTOR Alan Chan
DESIGNERS Alan Chan, Phillip Leung
CLIENT Obunsha Pacific Corp.
PRODUCT Dai Sen Tea House Menu
  and Take-Out Box

DESIGN FIRM
Design Ahead

DESIGNER
Ralf Stumpf

CLIENT
Design Ahead

PRODUCT
Self-promotion

This box, filled with the Design Ahead Gearwheel logo made of marzipan, was sent to special clients as a Christmas gift.

DESIGN FIRM
K-Products

ALL DESIGN
John Vander Stelt

CLIENT
Self-promotion

PRODUCT
Outbreak

This promotion introduced K-Products' new Outbreak Jacket. It was mailed to 378 buyers, and fifty-two placed orders for the new jackets. Details such as the pine scent pouch, colorful fall leaf, and brown tissue paper make this a memorable promotion.

DESIGN FIRM Hornall Anderson Design Works
ART DIRECTORS Jack Anderson, Julia Lapine
DESIGNERS Julia Lapine, Denise Weir, Lian Ng
ILLUSTRATOR Larry Jost
HAND LETTERING Nancy Stenz
CLIENT Puget Sound Marketing Corporation

DESIGN FIRM Graphic Partners
ART DIRECTOR Ken Craig
DESIGNER Kate Stockwell
CLIENT Baxter's
PRODUCT George Baxter's Cellar & Mrs. Baxter's
Victorian Kitchen Confectionary

PRODUCT Java Joe's Coffee
CLIENT Java Joe's
DESIGN FIRM Sayles Graphic Design
ART DIRECTOR John Sayles
DESIGNER John Sayles
ILLUSTRATOR John Sayles

DESIGN FIRM Muller and Company,
Kansas City, Missouri
DESIGNER Michelle Krauss
PRODUCT Bagel Street Café cream cheese

(opposite page)
DESIGN FIRM Newell and Sorrell, Ltd.,
London
CREATIVE DIRECTORS John Sorrell,
Frances Newell
DESIGNER Sarah Franks
ILLUSTRATOR Edward Bawden
CLIENT Cranks, London

DESIGN FIRM Addison Design Consultants Worldwide,
San Francisco, California
DESIGNERS Eileen Limsico and Micaela Mercé
PRODUCT C & H Magic Sugar

DESIGN FIRM B.E.P. Design Group
ART DIRECTOR Jean-Jacques Evrard
DESIGNER Carole Purnelle
CLIENT Paul Decamps
PRODUCT Mons & Merveilles

DESIGN FIRM Design Center
ART DIRECTOR John Reger
DESIGNER Kobe, Todd Spichick
CLIENT Lafayette Club
PRODUCT Identity Program

DESIGN FIRM Wallace Church Associates, Inc.
ART DIRECTOR Stanley Church/Robert Wallace
DESIGNER Phyllis Chan
CLIENT Ralph Lauren Home Collection
PRODUCT The Polo Sheet

(opposite page)

PRODUCT Wine (Cento Per Cento Chardonay)
CLIENT Viansa Winery
DESIGN FIRM Britton Design
ART DIRECTOR Patti Britton
DESIGNER Patti Britton
ILLUSTRATOR Evans & Brown
PHOTOGRAPHER Thea Schrack

DESIGN FIRM Trickett & Webb
DESIGNERS Lynn Trickett, Brian Webb, Avril Broadley
ILLUSTRATOR Trickett & Webb
CLIENT Dorma
PRODUCT Art of Living

PRODUCT Wine (Cento Per Cento Chardonay)
CLIENT Viansa Winery
DESIGN FIRM Britton Design
ART DIRECTOR Patti Britton
DESIGNER Patti Britton
ILLUSTRATOR Evans & Brown
PHOTOGRAPHER Thea Schrack

DESIGN FIRM Dil Consultants in Design
ART DIRECTORS Dil Design Team
CLIENT Fleischmann E. Royal, Nabisco
PRODUCT Petits Coeurs Cookies

DESIGN FIRM Dil Consultants in Design
ART DIRECTORS Dil Design Team
CLIENT Sadia Commercial S.A.
PRODUCT Sadia Ham and Liver Pate

DESIGN FIRM
Vanessa Eckstein

ALL DESIGN
Vanessa Eckstein

CLIENT
The Bag Stand Company

PRODUCT
Cosmetic cases

TECHNIQUE
Offset

This product is aimed at a teenage market. The design had to be playful, hip, and colorful. It's a "fun" product, and the design needed to express the energetic feeling of this young audience.

DESIGN FIRM Mires Design

DESIGNER José A. Serrano, Miguel Perez

ILLUSTRATOR Tracy Sabin

CLIENT Bordeaux Printers

PRODUCT Bordeaux printing services

This client wanted to communicate the image of high-end printing. Mires Design did this by printing labels and hang tags as part of a quality assurance program. The labels and tags were signed by sales representatives and production people to reassure clients that the printed samples had been carefully inspected.

DESIGN FIRM Louise Fili Ltd.
ART DIRECTOR/DESIGNER Louise Fili
CLIENT Chronicle Books
PRODUCT Greeting cards
TECHNIQUE Offset

This series of cards was produced by Chronicle Books by using the designer's collection of French advertising fans from the twenties and thirties.

(opposite page)
DESIGN FIRM Pentagram, New York, NY
PARTNER Peter Harrison
ASSOCIATE PARTNER AND DESIGNER
Susan Hauchbaum
ILLUSTRATOR Paul Davis

Graphic identity program for the 21 Club in New York includes logotype, history booklet, menu, banquet package, wine label and stationery. Through updating this traditonal landmark restaurant, the well-known '21' jockey remained a graphic reference to its history.

DESIGN FIRM Louise Fili Ltd.
ART DIRECTOR/DESIGNER Louise Fili
CLIENT El Paso Chile Co.
PRODUCT Floribunda
TECHNIQUE Offset

The challenge here was to find a way to package a kit of bulbs, soil, pot, and saucer. Louise Fili Ltd. came up with the name Floribunda and decided to make a tie-on tag that could include the copy.

DESIGN FIRM Pedersen Gesk

ART DIRECTOR Rony Zibara

DESIGNER Rony Zibara, Kris Morgan, Mark Orton

CLIENT Anchor Hocking Plastics

PRODUCT Kitchen Essentials

The design strategy here was to introduce a revolutionary line of plastic containers aimed at "food preparation" oriented households—homes where people spend a fair amount of time in the kitchen. The design highlights the different storage solutions, and the color scheme is French Country.

DESIGN FIRM Pedersen Gesk

ART DIRECTOR Mitch Lindgren

DESIGNER Kris Morgan

CLIENT Target

PRODUCT Pet Essentials food
and toys

This was the new private label design for Target Pet Essentials. The design appeals to the consumer's love for pets. The toys take the concept of the food packaging and add playfulness to the pets.

DESIGN FIRM Alternatives
ART DIRECTOR Julie Koch-Beinke
DESIGNER-PHOTOGRAPHER Kevin Yates
CLIENT Kiss My Face
PRODUCT Kiss My Face Moisture Bath

DESIGN FIRM The Joppa Group
ART DIRECTOR Bruce Demustchine
DESIGNER Irene Johnson
ILLUSTRATOR Elizabeth Golz Rush
CLIENT Pier 1 Imports
PRODUCT Kashmir

DESIGN FIRM FRCH Design Worldwide
ART DIRECTOR Joan Donnelly
DESIGNER Tim A. Frame
PHOTOGRAPHER Bray Ficken
CLIENT Aca Joe
PRODUCT Men's jeans
TECHNIQUE Four-color offset

These pocket flashers are used to communicate four types of jean fits for men's denim pants. Different images of women's lips were used to represent individual fits.

DESIGN FIRM FRCH Design Worldwide
ART DIRECTOR Joan Donnelly
DESIGNER Tim A. Frame
CLIENT Aca Joe
PRODUCT Men's chinos
TECHNIQUE Two-color offset
(one color plus timed varnish)

These waistband tickets are used to communicate two styles of men's basic chinos.

DESIGN FIRM Robilant & Associati

ART DIRECTOR Maurizio di Robilant

DESIGNER Lucia Sommaruga

CLIENT Koh-I-Noor Italy

PRODUCT Wood collection

The project's aim was to create natural, environmentally-friendly packaging for a line of combs and brushes made of natural materials (wood, hair). Instead of using acetate, the designers used drawings to represent the product contained in the box. The whole package needs only one glue point.

DESIGN FIRM Teikna

ART DIRECTOR/DESIGNER Claudia Neri

CLIENT Club Monaco

PRODUCT Jeans Tag

TECHNIQUE Offset

For their Fall '96 jeans, Club Monaco needed a design for their pant tags which would fit with the retailer's simple, modern image, and appeal to men. Artwork was done in QuarkXPress.

DESIGN FIRM Bunny Levy & Associates
ART DIRECTOR Bunny Levy, Paulette Lue
DESIGNER Paulette Lue
ILLUSTRATOR Cathy Diefendorf
  (Mendola Artists rep)
CLIENT Desnoes & Geddes Ltd.
PRODUCT Hampden Club Rums
TECHNIQUE Offset

Jamaica has a long tradition of rum making. As a new player, Desnoes and Geddes Ltd. sought to attract a new and younger rum drinking audience with a dynamic, contemporary design. Aldus Freehand and Adobe Photoshop were used.

DESIGN FIRM Bunny Levy & Associates
ART DIRECTOR Bunny Levy, Paulette Lue
DESIGNER Paulette Lue
ILLUSTRATOR Cathy Diefendorf,
  Joyce Kitchell, Larry Winborg
CLIENT Estate Industries
PRODUCT Lillifield liqueur
TECHNIQUE Offset

Illustrators with loose, painterly styles were chosen for this project. Each illustrator was given freedom with composition, color, and illustrative style. Embossing was used to further enhance areas of the illustrations as well as the typeface. Aldus Freehand and Adobe Photoshop were used.

DESIGN FIRM Michael Stanard
ART DIRECTOR Michael Stanard
DESIGNER Ann Werner
CLIENT Beatrice
PRODUCT Treasure Cave Brie

DESIGN FIRM Cato Gobe, New York, New York
PRODUCT Gillette shaving products

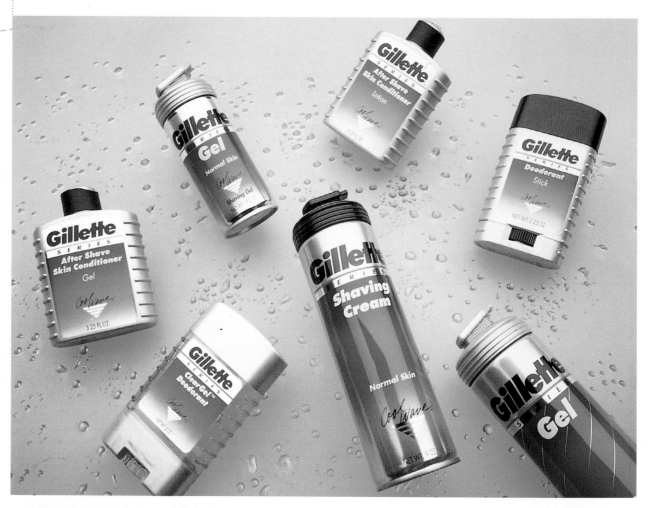

DESIGN FIRM The Design Company
ART DIRECTOR-DESIGNER Marcia Romanuck
PHOTOGRAPHER Chesapeake Studios
CLIENT Whaling Industries
PRODUCT Newport Harbor Menswear

DESIGN FIRM Barry Zaid Design,
  New York, New York
PACKAGE CONCEPT, PAINTING Barry Zaid
CLIENT Kleenex (Kimberly-Clark of
  Canada Ltd.

DESIGN FIRM P & B Communiçào, Brazil
ART DIRECTOR Joào Delpino
CLIENT Klabin Paper and Cellulose
  Manfacturers

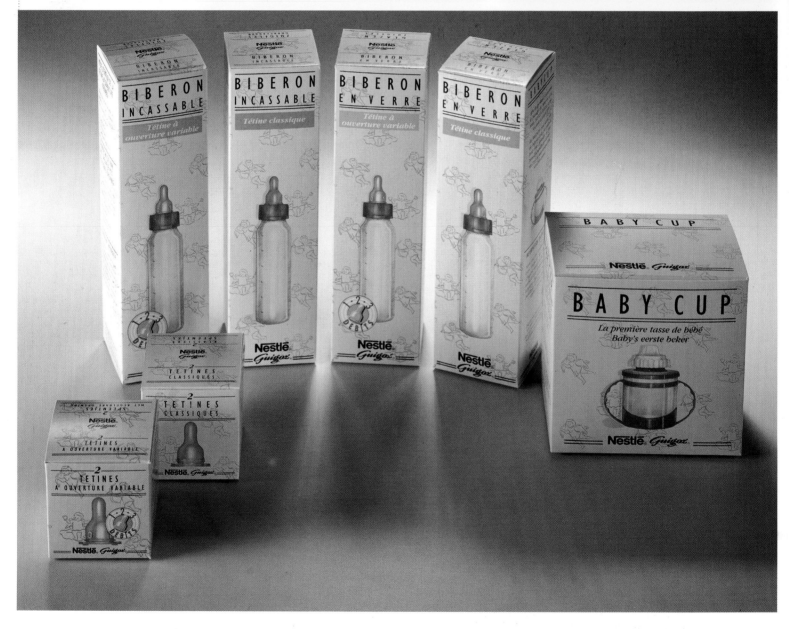

DESIGN FIRM Sibley-Peteet Design

ART DIRECTOR Bryan Jesse

DESIGNER/ILLUSTRATOR Rex Peteet

CLIENT Farah

PRODUCT Men's clothing

TECHNIQUE Offset, weaving

Sibley-Peteet Design embraced the existing equity of the typeface and updated the look with a contemporary and more fashionable treatment without turning off the older, existing market. The art was created with Adobe Illustrator.

DESIGN FIRM

Sibley-Peteet Design

ART DIRECTOR

Bryan Jesse, Rex Peteet

DESIGNER/ILLUSTRATOR

Rex Peteet, Derek Welch

CLIENT

Farah

PRODUCT

Men's clothing

TECHNIQUE

Offset, weaving

Sibley-Peteet Design created a new identity and image for a young, mobile market. The workplace is becoming more casual and Savane meets the need for fashion that is comfortable, good looking, and easy to care for. Many products in this line are wrinkle-free and stain resistant.

DESIGN FIRM Pentagram Design Inc.

ART DIRECTOR Paula Scher

DESIGNER Lisa Mazur

ILLUSTRATOR Paula Scher, Lisa Mazur

CLIENT G.H. Bass & Co./Spirit of Maine

PRODUCT Specialty gift items

TECHNIQUE Offset

*Spirit of Maine food, gardening, and gift products of
New England are sold exclusively in G.H. Bass & Co.
stores. Black-and-white maritime photographs
accentuate the sub-brand's Yankee personality
and origins.*

DESIGN FIRM Clark Design

ART DIRECTOR Annemarie Clark

DESIGNER Thurlow Washam

PHOTOGRAPHER Geoffrey Nelson

CLIENT Oracle

PRODUCT Video

TECHNIQUE Offset

*This video promotes the Oracle Channel, a division of
Oracle Education. The packaging needed to use the
same design that the firm had created for a brochure
announcing the product.*

DESIGN FIRM Hornall Anderson Design Works

ART DIRECTOR Jack Anderson

DESIGNERS Jack Anderson, Julia Lapine

ILLUSTRATOR Julia Lapine

CLIENT Italia Restaurants

DESIGN FIRM Hornall Anderson Design Works

ART DIRECTOR Jack Anderson

DESIGNERS Jack Anderson, Mary Hermes

ILLUSTRATOR Scott McDougal

CLIENT Broadmor Bakery

DESIGN FIRM Hornall Anderson Design Works
ART DIRECTOR Jack Anderson
DESIGNER Jack Anderson, Jana Nishi, Mary Hermes,
 Heidi Favour, David Bates, Mary Chin Hutchison
ILLUSTRATOR Keith Ward
CLIENT Seattle Chocolate Company
PRODUCT Seattle Chocolates

A family look was created by developing a black corrugated bottom to be used on all flavors. A combination of tip-ins, hot-stamping debossing, embossing, and matte and gloss varnishes were used to give the entire package the special feeling it needed for a gift box.

DESIGN FIRM Greteman Group
ART DIRECTOR Sonia Greteman, James Strange
DESIGNER/ILLUSTRATOR James Strange
CLIENT Menefee & Partners
PRODUCT Pizza

This fun Cafe Doskocil pizza box was used as a promotion to sell pizza toppings. The art is retro, using black and red for impact. It was created in Macromedia FreeHand.

DESIGN FIRM Shimokochi/Reeves
ART DIRECTOR Mamoru Shimokochi,
  Anne Reeves
DESIGNER Mamoru Shimokochi
ILLUSTRATOR Jim Krogle
CLIENT Leiner Health Products
PRODUCT Bodycology
TECHNIQUE Lithography

This is the brand identity and package
redesign for thirty-three body, bath, and
haircare products. To achieve maximum
shelf impact, Shimokochi/Reeves used
large, brightly-colored illustrations and
strengthened the Bodycology brand
logotype. The frosted containers and
floral images reflect each product's
natural ingredients and fragrance. The
art was created with Adobe Illustrator.

DESIGN FIRM Shimokochi/Reeves
CREATIVE DIRECTOR Mamoru Shimokochi, Anne Reeves
DESIGNER/ILLUSTRATOR Mamoru Shimokochi
CLIENT Dep Corporation
PRODUCT Nature's Family

This is a proposed brand identity and
package revitalization for a line of
natural ingredient–based skin care
products. The art was created with
Adobe Illustrator.

DESIGN FIRM Tucker Design, Eastwood, Australia
CREATIVE DIRECTOR AND PROJECT DESIGNER
Barrie Tucker
ASSISTANT DESIGNER AND PROJECT COORDINATOR
Joe Marrapodi
PRODUCT Saddler's Creek Sauternes and Muscat
dessert wines; labels made from 100% recycled
corrugated board

DESIGN FIRM Planet Design Company

ART DIRECTOR Dana Lytle, Kevin Wade

DESIGNER Kevin Wade, Martha Graettinger

CLIENT Lortex

PRODUCT Natural nylon fabric

TECHNIQUE Screen

This piece, used for presentation by the sales staff, tries to capture both the high tech and natural characteristics of the nylon. Macromedia FreeHand and QuarkXPress were used to create this design.

DESIGN FIRM Mittleman-Robinson Inc.
ART DIRECTOR-DESIGNER Fred Mittleman
CLIENT Vinos Argentinos
PRODUCT Trapiche wines

DESIGN FIRM Emery-Poe Design
ART DIRECTOR David Poe
DESIGNERS-ILLUSTRATORS David Poe, Jonathan Mulcare
CLIENT The Piedmont Grocery
PRODUCT Piedmont Grocery Labels

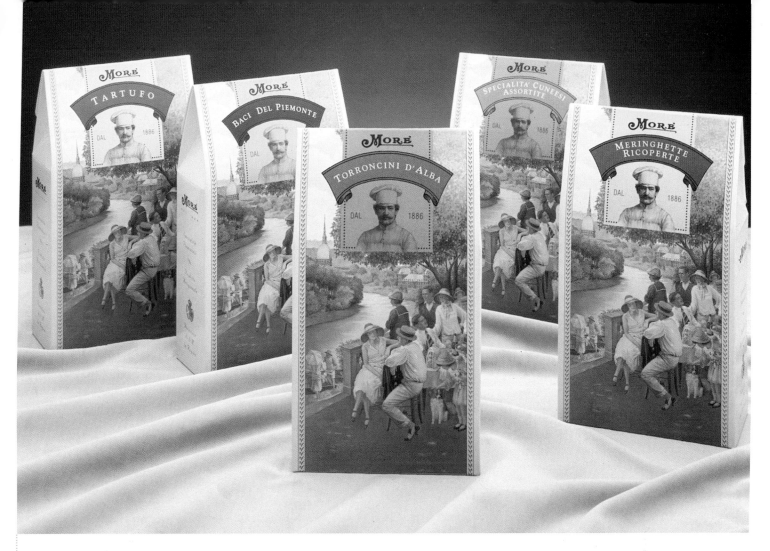

DESIGN FIRM Angelo Sganzerla

ART DIRECTOR/DESIGNER Angelo Sganzerla

ILLUSTRATOR Alfonso Goi

CLIENT Stainer

PRODUCT Pralines, meringues, nougats

*The watercolor illustration for this line of typical
Piedmontese sweets depicts a riverside festivity against
the background of Turin.*

DESIGN FIRM Angelo Sganzerla

ART DIRECTOR/DESIGNER Angelo Sganzerla

ILLUSTRATOR Alfonso Goi

CLIENT Solci

PRODUCT Modena Balsamic Vinegar

*Here are three gift packs of Modena Balsamic Vinegar,
the finest produced in Italy. The various colors on the
box correspond with the different prices according to
length of aging.*

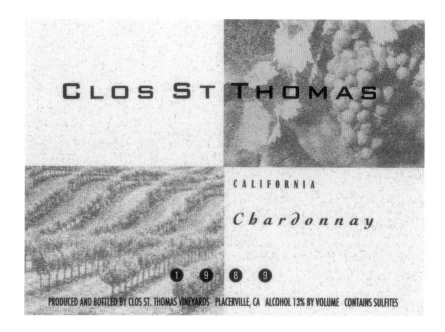

CALIFORNIA
Chardonnay

① ⑨ ⑧ ⑨

PRODUCED AND BOTTLED BY CLOS ST. THOMAS VINEYARDS PLACERVILLE, CA ALCOHOL 13% BY VOLUME CONTAINS SULFITES

DESIGN FIRM The Weller Institute For The Cure of Design
ART DIRECTOR Don Young
DESIGNERS Don Weller, Don Young
ILLUSTRATOR Don Weller
CLIENT Thomas Yeager

DESIGN FIRM Alan Chan Design Co.
ART DIRECTOR Alan Chan
DESIGNERS Alan Chan, Alvin Chan
CLIENT Heichinrou Restaurant
PRODUCT Heichinrou Restaurant
House Wine

DESIGN FIRM Watts Graphic Design

ART DIRECTOR/DESIGNER Helen and Peter Watts

CLIENT Watts Graphic Design

PRODUCT Christmas Gift

TECHNIQUE Laser print with foil

Every year Watts Graphic Design gives its clients a gift to show appreciation. This self-promotion was a great success. Clients called to comment on the unique design. It is simple but effective.

DESIGN FIRM
Rickabaugh Graphics
ART DIRECTOR
Eric Rickabaugh
DESIGNER
Mark Krumel
PHOTOGRAPHER
Larry Hamill
CLIENT
Cordage Papers (paper wholesaler)
PRODUCT
Paper sample swatch books
TECHNIQUE
Offset

In an effort to tie in the natural beginnings of paper, various photos and textures were scanned. All other graphics and the package system were created in Macromedia FreeHand. Box graphics were printed on light-weight paper, laminated, and wrapped onto the cardboard shell. The swatch book covers were printed on cover stock and laminated.

(opposite page)
DESIGN FIRM Alan Chan Design Company,
Wanchai, Hong Kong
CREATIVE DIRECTOR Alan Chan
DESIGNERS Alan Chan and Chen Shun Tsoi
PRODUCT Alkaff Mansion spices,
sold in Singapore

DESIGN FIRM Clark Design
ART DIRECTOR Annemarie Clark
DESIGNER Craig Stout
CLIENT Clark Design
PRODUCT Holiday card/gift
   of beeswax candles
TECHNIQUE Xerox, hand-cut

This holiday card/gift of beeswax candles is wrapped in soft corrugated stock. A poem about the gift of light spirals around the outside of the corrugated stock. It is mailed in a tube. The design was created in QuarkXPress.

DESIGN FIRM Animus Comunicação

ART DIRECTOR Rique Nitzsche

DESIGNER Felicio Torres

CLIENT Animus Comunicação

PRODUCT Christmas gift

TECHNIQUE Inkjet

This Christmas promotional gift was designed on the computer and printed on an inkjet color printer. The labels were hand-located by the Animus Comunicação staff. All of the labels were personalized with the name of the person who received the gift.

DESIGN FIRM Hornall Anderson Design Works
ART DIRECTOR Jack Anderson
DESIGNERS Jack Anderson, Julia Lapine
ILLUSTRATOR Julia Lapine
CLIENT Italia
PRODUCT Italia Restaurant Bags

CHOCOLATE
MINT
ALMONDS

CRUNCHY, WHOLE,
TOASTED CALIFORNIA
ALMONDS LAVISHLY
COATED WITH RICH
BITTERSWEET CHOCO-
LATE AND FINISHED
WITH MINTED WHITE
CHOCOLATE.

COCOLAT
BERKELEY, CALIFORNIA 94710

COCOLAT

BITTERSWEET
CHOCOLATE
RAISIN BARK

SWEET, SUNRIPENED
RAISINS IN RICH, BIT-
TERSWEET CHOCOLATE
FOR CONNOISSEURS AND
SERIOUS NIBBLERS.
IRRESISTIBLE.

COCOLAT
BERKELEY, CALIFORNIA 94710

TRIPLE
CHOCOLATE
ALMONDS

CRUNCHY, WHOLE,
FRESH TOASTED CALI-
FORNIA ALMONDS LAV-
ISHLY COATED WITH
RICH, BITTERSWEET
AND MILK CHOCOLATES
AND DUSTED WITH THE
FINEST DUTCH COCOA.

COCOLAT
BERKELEY, CALIFORNIA 94710

(opposit page)

DESIGN FIRM Morla Design, San Francisco, California

ART DIRECTOR Jennifer Morla

CREATIVE DIRECTOR Jennifer Morla

DESIGNER Jennifer Morla

Recycled, reusable paper was used for the packaging of Cocolat Gourmet chocolates.

DESIGN FIRM

Ian Logan Design Company, London

ART DIRECTORS Ian Logan, Stuart Gates, Harrods

DESIGNER Alan Colville

ILLUSTRATOR Brian Cook

Package designs for a variety of traditional Harrods biscuits

DESIGN FIRM

Barrie Tucker Design Pty, Ltd., Eastwood, Australia

ART DIRECTOR-DESIGNER

Barrie Tucker

DESIGNER-ILLUSTRATOR-TYPOGRAPHER Jody Tucker

Presentation design for Morris of Rutherglen Fortfied Wines. The design program incorporates the history and tradition of the company in an attractive gift packaging.

DESIGN FIRM The Design Company
ART DIRECTOR Marcia Romanuck
DESIGNER/ILLUSTRATOR Marcia Romanuck, Busha Husak
CLIENT Habersham Winery
PRODUCT Habersham wine
TECHNIQUE Offset, four-color PMS

This was an existing product line that needed a more
sophisticated look to match the quality of the wine. The
art was illustrated by hand and scanned into a Quark
document.

DESIGN FIRM Lewis Moberly
ART DIRECTOR/DESIGNER Mary Lewis
CLIENT Arnold Dettling
PRODUCT Dettling Kirschwasser

Kirsch typically is packaged in clear flint standard bottles,
but Dettling wanted to break the mold and design a
unique bottle. The colored glass reflects the deep stain of
black cherries. The slim bottle has a flat back and curved
front with an applied label only on the neck. The brand's
credentials are in hand-drawn clear script against a frosted
surface.

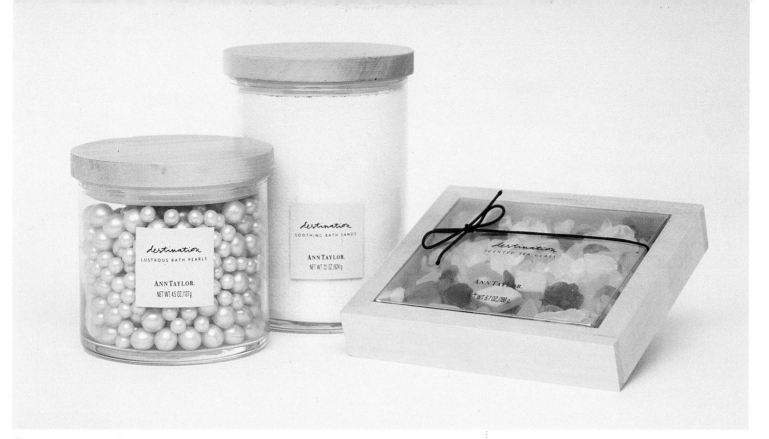

DESIGN FIRM Desgrippes Gobé & Associates
CREATIVE DIRECTOR Peter Levine, Kenneth Hirst
DESIGN DIRECTOR Frances Ullenberg
DESIGNER Christopher Freas
CLIENT Ann Taylor Inc.
PRODUCT Ann Taylor Destination fragrance

This packaging reinforces the Ann Taylor brand identity by communicating a natural, honest design that is consistent with the store's total retail identity. The fragrance packaging's materials are made from recycled and recyclable materials and have soft, nature-based shapes.

DESIGN FIRM Sibley-Peteet Design
ART DIRECTOR Bryan Jesse, Rex Peteet
DESIGNER Rex Peteet, Derek Welch
ILLUSTRATOR Stephen Alcorn
CLIENT Farah
PRODUCT Men's clothing
TECHNIQUE Offset, weaving

Sibley-Peteet Design created a new identity for a younger market. The client wanted a solid, bold, simple feel. Woodcuts were scanned into Adobe Illustrator.

DESIGN FIRM Tharp Did It
ART DIRECTOR Rick Tharp
DESIGNER Jana Heer, Colleen Sullivan and RickTharp
PHOTOGRAPHER Kelly O'Connor
CLIENT Service Through Touch
PRODUCT Massage Oil

(opposite page)
DESIGN FIRM Trickett & Webb
DESIGNERS Brian Webb, Lynn Trickett, Avril Broadley,
  Sarah Mattinson
ILLUSTRATORS Glynn Boyd Hart, Paul Leith
CLIENT Tesco

TESCO

ORGANICALLY

g r o w n

P R O D U C E

TESCO CAN NOW OFFER YOU NATURALLY GROWN
PRODUCE FROM AROUND THE WORLD.

OUR ORGANIC FRUITS AND VEGETABLES ARE GROWN
TO STANDARDS MONITORED BY TESCO AND THE
ORGANIC GROWERS SOIL ASSOCIATION IN FIELDS AND
ORCHARDS FREE FROM ARTIFICIAL CHEMICAL PESTI-
CIDES AND FERTILIZERS FOR AT LEAST TWO YEARS.

THE TESCO RANGE IS GROWN USING NATURAL COMPOST
FERTILIZERS AND IS IDEAL FOR THOSE CONCERNED
ABOUT CHEMICAL RESIDUES AND THE ENVIRONMENT.

THE PRODUCE HAS A NATURAL APPEARANCE AND IS A
LITTLE MORE EXPENSIVE THAN OUR CONVENTIONAL
RANGE. THIS IS BECAUSE IT IS MORE DIFFICULT TO
GROW CROPS USING ONLY NATURAL METHODS.

TRY OUR NEW RANGE BY
LOOKING OUT FOR THIS LOGO

DESIGN FIRM Graphic Partners
ART DIRECTOR Ken Craig & Graham Duffy
DESIGNER Mark Ross & Andrea Welsh
ILLUSTRATOR Colin Backhouse
CLIENT Msarks & Spencer
PRODUCT Marks & Spencer Bread

DESIGN FIRM Tangram Strategic Design
ART DIRECTOR Enrico Sempi-Antonella Trevisan
DESIGNER Antonella Trevisan
ILLUSTRATOR Sergio Quaranta
CLIENT E. Vismara di Antonio Biffi
PRODUCT Sughi D'Autore

DESIGN FIRM The Design Company
ART DIRECTOR Marcia Romanuck
DESIGNERS Marcia Romanuck, Denise Pickering
PHOTOGRAPHY Chespeake Studios
CLIENT Baldwin Hill

To see more beautiful work by these designers and
more, see these books from Rockport Publishers:

Great Package Design

Great Package Design 2

International Brand Packaging Awards 2

Label Design 3

Label Design 4

Package and Label Design